# *Irish* AMERICANS

SPIRIT
of America®

# *Irish* AMERICANS

By Sarah E. De Capua

The Child's World®
Chanhassen, Minnesota

# *Irish* AMERICANS

**Published in the United States of America by The Child's World®**
PO Box 326 • Chanhassen, MN 55317-0326 • 800-599-READ • www.childsworld.com

*Acknowledgments*
The Child's World®: Mary Berendes, Publishing Director

Editorial Directions, Inc.: E. Russell Primm, Emily Dolbear, Sarah E. De Capua, and Lucia Raatma, Editors; Linda S. Koutris, Photo Selector; Image Select International, Photo Research; Red Line Editorial and Pam Rosenberg, Fact Research; Tim Griffin/IndexServ, Indexer; Chad Rubel, Proofreader

*Photos*
Cover/frontispiece: An Irish-American family arriving in New York City in 1929

Cover photographs ©: Corbis/Bettmann; Tim Thompson/Corbis

Interior photographs ©: Library of Congress, Prints and Photographs Division, Detroit Publishing Company Collection, 6; Corbis, 7 top; AKG-Images, Berlin, 7 bottom; Getty Images, 8, 9, 10; Corbis, 11; Getty Images, 12; Corbis, 13; Ann Ronan Picture Library, 15; Getty Images, 16; Gamma/C. Halebain, 17; Corbis, 18, 19 top, 19 bottom, 20, 21, 22, 23; TRIP/H.Rogers, 23, 24; Gamma/Giboux, 25 top; AKG-Images, Berlin, 25 bottom; Corbis, 26; Ann Ronan Picture Library, 27; Getty Images, 28 top; Getty Images/Eyewire, 28 bottom.

*Registration*
The Child's World®, Spirit of America®, and their associated logos are the sole property and registered trademarks of The Child's World®.

*Library of Congress Cataloging-in-Publication Data*
De Capua, Sarah.
  Irish Americans / by Sarah DeCapua.
    p. cm.
  Includes bibliographical references and index.
  Summary: Provides information on the background, heritage, and traditions of Irish Americans.
  ISBN 1-56766-155-6
  1. Irish Americans—Juvenile literature. [1. Irish Americans.] I. Title.
  E184.I6 D38 2002
  973'.049162—dc21
                                2001007821

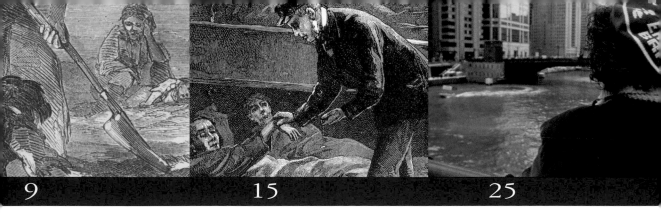

9 15 25

# *Contents*

# Chapter ONE

# A New Land

The S.S. Nevada, *the ship on which Annie Moore sailed to America*

SHE STOOD BETWEEN HER TWO YOUNGER brothers at the railing of the S.S. *Nevada*. She held their hands and looked up at the Statue of Liberty as the ship sailed into New York Harbor. After many weeks at sea, she had finally reached America. It felt good to be up on deck in the fresh air, even though it was cold. She was excited to see her parents, who would be waiting for her and her brothers when the ship docked. But she was also a little afraid. What would the United States be like? Would she make friends? Would she ever see her home in Ireland again?

A statue of Annie Moore and her younger brothers stands on Ellis Island today.

The girl's name was Annie Moore. She arrived in the United States on January 1, 1892, her 15th birthday. She was the first immigrant to be processed through Ellis Island. Ellis Island is located between New York and New Jersey. The headquarters there was open from 1892 to 1954. During those years, about 12 million immigrants were accepted into the United States through Ellis Island. Annie was the first immigrant to go through Ellis Island. But she wasn't the first Irish immigrant to the United States. The Irish had been coming to the United States for more than 100 years before Annie's arrival.

The lush, green land of Ireland

7

Ireland is a small country in northwestern Europe. It is about the size of the U.S. state of Maine. The Atlantic Ocean borders Ireland on three sides. The Irish Sea lies along the fourth side. Ireland's climate is wet and rainy. As a result, the land is dark green in color. Legend says that 40 shades of green can be found in Ireland's countryside. Ireland is known throughout the world as the Emerald Isle.

*Farming was a way of life for many families in Ireland.*

For much of Ireland's history, its lush land has been used for farming. In the 1800s, large farms called estates covered Ireland. These estates were owned by wealthy British people. The British had conquered Ireland in 1171. The Irish rented land from the British to live and farm on. By the mid-1800s, most Irish people were poor **peasants** living in small villages on the estates.

Potatoes were the major crop grown on these estates. They became an important part of the Irish diet because they are **nutritious**

8

and easy to grow, requiring very little farm-work. Also, potatoes can be cooked in many different ways. For years, most Irish peasants ate almost nothing but potatoes.

In 1845, however, a disease called potato blight destroyed half of Ireland's potato crop. The blight caused the stalks and leaves of potato plants to be covered with brown and black spots. The potatoes, which grow underground, were black and mushy. It happened again in 1846. Ireland's potato crop either rotted in the ground or shortly after **harvesting**. Except for 1847, the potato blight destroyed Ireland's potato crop for the next ten years. Without their most important food source, the people starved. These years

*An Irish woman and her children searching the ground for potatoes during the Great Hunger*

## Interesting Fact

▸ The voyage from Ireland to the United States took between one month and three months.

are known in Ireland as the Great Hunger. Outside Ireland, that period is known as the Irish Potato Famine. About 1 million of Ireland's 8 million people starved to death or died of diseases related to the famine.

The British government offered some help by opening soup kitchens, but these were not enough to feed the millions of Irish who were starving. After a while, the Irish became desperate. It became clear to them that their only hope for survival was to leave Ireland. Leaving villages, families, and friends was very hard. Most knew they would never see their homeland or loved ones again. Those who left Ireland out of desperation also felt hope for a brighter future in the United States. From 1845 to 1855, 1.5 million Irish people emigrated to the United States.

*Food being prepared at a soup kitchen during the years of the Great Hunger*

10

IT RAINS A LOT IN IRELAND. DURING THE SUMMER OF 1846, HOWEVER, IT rained much more than usual. Some days started out warm and sunny. But huge clouds moved in over the land in the afternoons. The days became chilly and damp. The rain fell for several hours at a time.

When the clouds moved in, the land became strangely silent. Birds stopped singing. Herds of sheep and cows stood still. At night, the wind blew the clouds away. A light frost left behind on the potato plants added to the destruction of the potato crop. The Irish called the clouds they dreaded the "potato fog."

# Chapter Two

# "No Irish Need Apply"

*A group of Irish citizens leaving their native country in 1895 for a new start in the United States*

BEFORE THE MID-1800S, THE FEW IRISH WHO came to the United States were mostly skilled, middle-class workers. They blended easily into the communities where they settled. They were accepted as upstanding citizens. By the mid-1800s, however, the number of Irish immigrants coming to the United States was overwhelming. Many were unskilled peasants who arrived penniless. Those who survived the difficult voyage across the Atlantic faced

more challenges when they arrived in the United States.

Many Irish people believed the United States was a place where everyone prospered. They thought there was plenty of food for everyone and a job for anyone who wanted to work. These Irish immigrants found that the United States was a very different place from the one they had imagined.

*Many Irish immigrants had to live in crowded, noisy apartment buildings.*

The first task of an Irish immigrant was finding a place to live. Most had little or no money, so they were forced to crowd into a dirty basement or a filthy apartment in a run-down building. These buildings were usually located in the **slums** of large cities. Often, several Irish families shared the same tiny living space. Basements often flooded. The apartments had no heat and no running water. There were no windows for sunlight or fresh air. The toilets were usually outside behind the building. Sometimes hundreds of people shared just a few toilets and sinks. These filthy conditions often led to deadly diseases. Fires were common. And the Irish still did not have enough food to eat.

Life in the slums was hard. Finding a job was almost impossible. The Irish who arrived in the United States before the potato famine were welcomed and respected for their willingness to work hard. The great numbers of Irish who fled the famine, however, were not welcome. Now there were too many workers and not enough jobs. American citizens and other immigrant groups feared that the Irish would steal their jobs. They started to believe the rumors that the Irish were lazy and dishonest. Signs that said "No Irish Need Apply" began to appear in the windows of stores and businesses with jobs to fill. Well-paid work was nearly impossible to find. Only the most dangerous, difficult, and **menial** jobs were available to Irish workers. Most Irishwomen worked as maids. Irishmen cleaned stables, unloaded cargo from ships, dug ditches, and laid railroad tracks.

The Irish did not allow poverty and **prejudice** to overwhelm them. They continued to work hard and to educate themselves. They believed in their own ability to overcome **adversity**.

14

MANY PEOPLE IN THE UNITED STATES THOUGHT THE IRISH WERE LAZY. They spread rumors that the Irish did not want to work. Those people did not realize that many Irish immigrants who arrived in the

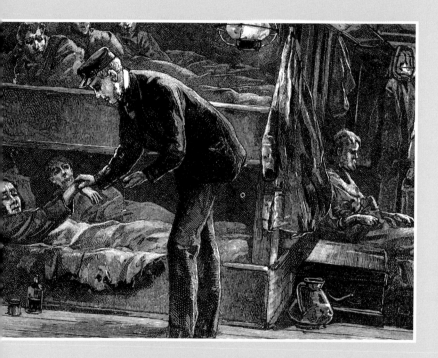

United States were still ill from their voyage. The trip across the Atlantic was long and difficult. Often, hundreds of immigrants were crowded into small areas below deck (left). The areas were built to hold cargo, not people. The travelers had no sinks, no fresh water, and no toilets. They did not have enough food or fresh air. People who had never sailed on the ocean became terribly seasick. The filthy conditions bred diseases that spread throughout the already-weakened immigrants. Cholera, dysentery, and typhoid were common. Many people died on the voyage to the United States. Others who lived to reach America remained ill. They could not get good medical care. As a result, it was more difficult for immigrants to keep the jobs they could find. It was nearly impossible to be so ill and still keep up with the hard, physical labor these jobs required. When their poor health held them back, they were thought of as lazy.

15

# Chapter THREE

# Making Their Own Way

*Tammany Hall, the head-
quarters of the Democratic
Party in New York City*

THE IRISH HAD TWO ADVANTAGES OVER OTHER immigrant groups. Although Gaelic was their native language, the British had tried to keep them from speaking it. As a result, the Irish immigrants already spoke English. Another advantage was their under-standing of the American political system, which was very much like Ireland's. One

of the first places the Irish found acceptance was in the world of politics.

By 1850, Irish Americans made up a large percentage of the population of New York City and Boston. Their numbers made them important to politicians running for public office in those cities. By the end of the 1850s, Irish Americans were influencing local politics in their own neighborhoods. By the 1860s, they controlled Tammany Hall, the headquarters of the Democratic Party in New York City. By the 1870s, they were electing members of the U.S. **Congress**. And, by the

*Many Irish people became police officers, like these marching in a Saint Patrick's Day parade in New York City.*

*The Irish also found work as firefighters in many U.S. cities.*

1890s, many large U.S. cities, such as Boston, Buffalo, Chicago, New York, Philadelphia, and San Francisco, were governed by Irish-American politicians.

Irish Americans knew the importance of being united. Many of them joined the Democratic Party. They worked to elect other Irish Americans to office. As a result, they were hired for city jobs. Many became police officers and firefighters. Over the years, as Irish Americans found steady, good-paying jobs, their living conditions improved. They moved out of the slums. By 1950, many Irish Americans lived in towns outside large cities. They owned their own homes. Today, Irish Americans can be found in almost every job in the United States.

Some Irish immigrants also joined the military. During the American Civil War

(1861–1865), large numbers of Irish men enlisted in the U.S. Army. Military life allowed them to show their fellow soldiers that they were neither lazy nor dishonest. They also showed their **patriotism**. American citizens serving with them were impressed by their bravery and skill on the battlefield.

Irish-American photographer Mathew Brady gained fame during the Civil War. His photographs of American history are in many cases the only record of key events in the 1800s. He and his staff of nearly 100 cameramen recorded the battles of the Civil War as well as images of army camp life.

*A portrait of Mathew Brady, a well-known photographer during the 1800s*

*Brigadier General Thomas Francis Meagher, commander of the Irish Brigade during the Civil War*

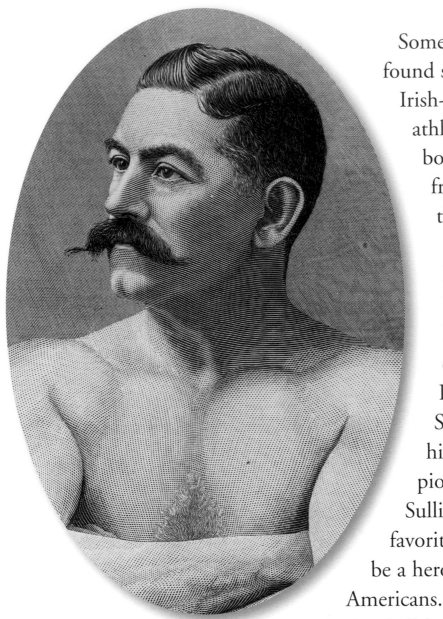

*John L. Sullivan gained fame as a boxer and was a hero to Irish crowds.*

Some Irish Americans found success in sports. Irish-American athletes dominated boxing and baseball from the 1860s to the 1920s.

One famous Irish-American boxer was John L. Sullivan. After defeating fighter Paddy Ryan, Sullivan declared himself the champion of the world. Sullivan was a crowd favorite and proved to be a hero for Irish Americans.

Baseball legend Connie Mack was the son of Irish immigrants. Born Cornelius Alexander McGillicuddy, Mack was a tall, lanky player who went on to gain fame as a manager. He had a reputation for building great clubs and luring key players to his teams. He was part owner and manager of the Philadelphia Athletics from 1900 to 1950, and he was named to the National Baseball Hall of Fame in 1937.

As more Americans came to admire these and other athletes, **discrimination** against the Irish decreased.

*Legendary baseball manager Connie Mack (right) with his son, Connie Jr., a player for the Philadelphia Athletics*

The Roman Catholic Church is an important part of Irish life. The Irish have strong Catholic beliefs. In the 1830s and 1840s, the Catholic Church in the United States was small. But when the Irish began arriving in large numbers, they built thousands of Catholic churches in the United States. Many of the churches included schools where Irish Americans sent their children. Irish Americans soon dominated the Catholic Church. Each year, hundreds of priests came from Ireland to serve in American parishes. In 1875, John McCloskey (right), the son of Irish

immigrants, was named by the pope as the first American cardinal. By 1900, half the bishops in the United States were of Irish descent. Today, the priests and bishops of the Catholic Church in the United States continue to be mostly Americans of Irish ancestry.

Saint Patrick's Cathedral in New York City (left) is perhaps the best-known Catholic church in the United States. Built by the Irish from 1858 to 1879, it stands as a reminder of the importance of the Catholic Church in the lives of Irish immigrants and their **descendants**.

# Chapter FOUR

# Successes and Contributions

*Saint Patrick, the patron saint of Ireland*

TODAY, IRISH AMERICANS ARE SO COMPLETELY accepted in society that most just call themselves "Americans." But Irish Americans have contributed to American culture in many ways.

Perhaps the best-known contribution is the holiday known as Saint Patrick's Day. In the 400s, Saint Patrick introduced Christianity to the people of Ireland. Today, he is the **patron saint** of Ireland. Saint Patrick is believed to have died on March 17, 461. In Ireland, March 17 is a national holiday. Every year on that day, people throughout the world who trace their roots to Ireland celebrate Saint Patrick's Day. They wear green, the color of Ireland, march in parades, and enjoy

Irish food.
Traditional Irish
food includes
corned beef and
cabbage with
potatoes, and
Irish stew.

In politics,
Alfred E. Smith
was the first Irish-American Catholic to run
for U.S. president. He was the Democratic
Party's nominee in the 1928 election. Although
he was defeated, he helped to bring Irish-
American politicians into the spotlight. In
1960, John F. Kennedy, whose great-grandfather
had emigrated from
Ireland, became the
first Irish-American
Catholic elected pres-
ident of the United
States. Many other
Irish Americans have
been influential in
American politics.

And the U.S.
Supreme Court has

*One way Chicago celebrates
Saint Patrick's Day is by dying
the Chicago River green.*

*President John F. Kennedy,
the great-grandson of Irish
immigrants*

boasted a number of Irish-American justices, including William J. Brennan Jr., Joseph McKenna, and Sandra Day O'Connor.

An important artist of the 20th century was Georgia O'Keeffe. The granddaughter of Irish immigrants, O'Keeffe was the first American woman painter to gain respect from both critics and the public. Known for her large flower paintings and her images of the American Southwest, she remains one of the most highly regarded American artists of all time.

Irish Americans have also had an impact on the U.S. stage and screen. James Cagney starred in *Yankee Doodle Dandy*, which was based on the life of Irish-American composer George M. Cohan. Other actors of Irish background include Bing Crosby, Gene Kelly, Jackie Gleason, Helen Hayes, and Grace Kelly, who went on to become the princess of Monaco. And for 22 years, American audiences enjoyed watching Irish-American Ed Sullivan host his television variety show.

A 1938 film titled *Boys Town* featured the life of a famous Irish American named Edward Joseph

*Grace Kelly and Bing Crosby, both Irish-American actors*

Flanagan. He was born in Ballymoe, Ireland, and later became a Catholic priest in Nebraska. Father Flanagan was interested in helping children who were homeless or in trouble. And he founded Boys Town in 1917 as a community for boys of all races and religions.

Irish-American writers have contributed great works of literature. Irish-American Eugene O'Neill was considered to be the greatest playwright of the 1900s. His works won four **Pulitzer Prizes** as well as the 1936 **Nobel Prize** for literature.

F. Scott Fitzgerald was believed to be one of the best novelists of the 1900s. Other well-known Irish-American writers include James T. Farrell, Mary Gordon, Maureen Howard, Flannery O'Connor, and Frank McCourt.

Irish folk dancing has become one of the most recognizable forms of entertainment today. The unique step dancing requires dancers to hold their arms at their sides while moving only their legs and feet. Irish dancing has been made popular by dancers such as Michael

*Eugene O'Neill, considered to be the greatest playwright of the 1900s*

*Adam Clayton, the Edge, and Bono (left to right), members of the Irish rock band U2*

Flatley and dance troupes such as the Trinity Dancers. In addition, musical groups such as U2 and the Chieftains have entertained audiences throughout the world.

Many Americans do not know that commonly used words have their origins in Gaelic, the language of the Irish. *Shamrock* and *leprechaun* are Gaelic words. *Bother* comes from a word that means "deaf." Its meaning has changed to "disturbing" or "annoying." The word *galore* means "enough" in Gaelic. Now it means "a lot" or "in large numbers."

*The shamrock, a symbol of Ireland, got its name from a Gaelic word.*

Irish immigrants overcame great difficulties to make important contributions to American society. It is no wonder that Americans whose ancestors left Ireland for a better life in the United States are so proud of their origins in the Emerald Isle.

*400 B.C* Celtic tribes invade Ireland.

*A.D 432* Saint Patrick brings Christianity to Ireland.

*1171* The British conquer Ireland and take over its lands.

*1800s* The Irish live and farm on British estates in Ireland.

*1801* Ireland becomes part of the United Kingdom of Great Britain and Ireland.

*1845–1846* The potato blight destroys half of Ireland's potato crop.

*1845–1855* More than half of Ireland's population is lost to death, disease, and emigration. Most emigrants choose America as their new home.

*1850* Irish immigrants make up a large portion of the populations of New York City and Boston.

*1860* Irish immigrants begin making significant contributions to American politics.

*1861–1865* The American Civil War is fought and many Irish immigrants serve with honor.

*1875* Irish-American John McCloskey is named as the first American cardinal of the Roman Catholic Church.

*1879* Saint Patrick's Cathedral in New York City is completed.

*1890s* Many of America's largest cities are governed by Irish-American politicians.

*1892* Ellis Island opens.

*1917* Father Flanagan founds Boys Town near Omaha, Nebraska, to help boys who are homeless and in trouble. It later becomes Girls and Boys Town.

*1928* Alfred E. Smith is the first Irish-American Catholic to run for president of the United States.

*1937* Baseball legend Connie Mack is named to the National Baseball Hall of Fame.

*1960* Irish-American John F. Kennedy is elected president of the United States.

*1980s* Many Irish living outside Ireland begin to return to their homeland. Descendants of Irish immigrants also begin moving to Ireland to live permanently.

**adversity (ad-VUHR-suh-tee)**
Adversity is hardship or misfortune. Many Irish Americans overcame adversity to succeed in the United States.

**Congress (KONG-griss)**
The U.S. Congress is that part of the U.S. government that makes laws. It is made up of the House of Representatives and the Senate. Irish Americans helped vote many members of Congress into office.

**descendants (dih-SEND-uhnts)**
Your descendants are your children, grand-children, and so on. A large number of American citizens today are descendants of Irish immigrants.

**discrimination (diss-krim-ih-AY-shuhn)**
Discrimination is unjust behavior toward others based on such differences as nationality, race, age, or other factors. In the mid-1800s, Irish Americans faced discrimination in the United States.

**harvesting (HAR-vist-ing)**
Harvesting is the gathering of ripe crops. During the potato blight, potatoes in Ireland rotted in the ground or shortly after harvesting.

**menial (MEEN-yuhl)**
A menial task is one that gets no respect. Upon their arrival in America, many Irish people had to take menial jobs.

**Nobel Prize (noh-BEL PRIZE)**
Nobel Prizes are international awards given each year for excellence in literature, economics, medicine, physics, chemistry, and for promoting peace. Eugene O'Neill won the Nobel Prize for literature in 1936.

**nutritious (noo-TRISH-uhs)**
A nutritious substance helps the body stay strong and healthy. The potato is a nutritious food that the Irish depended on.

**patriotism (PAY-tree-uht-ism)**
Patriotism is love for one's country and a willing-ness to fight for it. Irish Americans showed their patriotism by serving in the military.

**patron saint (PAY-truhn SAYNT)**
A specific saint who is believed to look after a certain country or group of people. Saint Patrick is the patron saint of Ireland.

**peasants (PEZ-uhnts)**
Peasants are people of low social status who usually work on farms. Many Irish people were peasants in their homeland.

**prejudice (PREJ-uh-diss)**
Prejudice is the hatred or unfair treatment of others based on such differences as nationality and race. The Irish did not allow prejudice to keep them from loving their new home in the United States.

**Pulitzer Prizes (puh-LIT-sur PRIZE-ez)**
Pulitzer Prizes are given each year to award excellence in writing. Eugene O'Neill won four Pulitzer Prizes.

**slums (sluhmz)**
Slums are overcrowded, poor, and neglected areas in a town or city. Many Irish immigrants had to live in slums when they first arrived in the United States.

# For Further INFORMATION

## Internet Sites

Visit our homepage for lots of links about Irish Americans:
**http://www.childsworld.com/links.html**

*Note to Parents, Teachers, and Librarians:*
We routinely verify our Web links to make sure they're safe,
active sites—so encourage your readers to check them out!

## Books

Bunting, Eve. *Dreaming of America: An Ellis Island Story.* Mahwah, N.J.: Troll, 2000.

Denenberg, Barry. *So Far from Home: The Diary of Mary Driscoll, an Irish Mill Girl.* New York: Scholastic, 1998.

January, Brendan. *Ireland.* Danbury, Conn.: Children's Press, 1999.

Miller, Kerby, and Patricia Mulholland Miller. *Journey of Hope: The Story of Irish Immigration to America.* San Francisco: Chronicle Books, 2001.

## Places to Visit or Contact

**The American Irish Historical Society**
991 Fifth Avenue
New York, NY 10028
212-288-2263

**Irish American Center**
4626 North Knox Avenue
Chicago, IL 60630
773-282-7035

**The Irish American Heritage Museum**
2267 Route 145
East Durham, NY 12423
518-634-7497

# Index